101 Powerful & Practical
Motivational Quotations & Daily Affirmations

101 Gems Of Greatness

101 Gems of Greatness
A Noval Idea Publishing Book
A subsidiary of A Noval Idea Inc.
P.O. Box 27242
Tampa, FL. 33623
© Copyright 2002 by Delatorro L. McNeal, II
All rights reserved: including the rights of reproduction in whole or in part in any form, except by newspaper or magazine reviews who wish to quote brief passages in connection with a review. No other part of this publication may be reproduced, stored in retrieval system, or transmitted in any form by any means electronic, mechanical, photocopying, recording or otherwise without prior written or expressed permissions of A Noval Idea Inc., A Noval Idea Publishing, or Delatorro L. McNeal, II.
Library of Congress Card Catalog No. 2002107150
ISBN # 0-9721324-0-6

Cover Design: Melanie Steen
Page Design & Typography: Melanie Steen
Photography: David Burgess
Literary Consultant: J. Ricc Rollins
PRINTED IN THE UNITED STATES OF AMERICA
FIRST NOVAL IDEA PUBLISHING: June 2002
This book is available at quantity discounts for bulk purchases. For additional information regarding A NOVAL IDEA, INC. visit us on the web at http://www.delmcneal.com/ or email us at INFO@DELMCNEAL.COM,
or call us at 1-866-GRATNES (1-866-472-8637)

101 Gems of Greatness

101 Powerful & Practical
Motivational Quotations & Daily Affirmations

Other Empowering Products Include:

101 Gems of Greatness "The Audio Book"
Foreword by Les Brown
Available in the Fall of 2002

Keys to Unlocking Your Greatness Audio Project
Introduction by Willie Jolley

The Power Principles for Empowering Families
LIVE Video
Also available on Audio

Addicted to Your Destiny LIVE Audio Project
Workbook Included

7 Steps to Greatness LIVE Audio Project
Workbook Included

Are You Willing LIVE Audio Project
Worksheet Included

Dedication Page

I dedicate this book and its impact to the one who made it all possible. The Lord Jesus Christ is my all and all, and I dedicate this book, my first book, to Him. Without Him, I would never be great, and neither would you; however, because of Him I can, you can, and we can accomplish all things!

101 Gems Of Greatness

Acknowledgements Page

To "The Queen" my beautiful, blessed, and virtuous wife Nova Taylor McNeal. You are my earth, my heaven-sent angel, and my partner for life. Thanks for being there for me ALL the time and helping me to help others live their dreams. My success is our success!

To my earthly creators, my mom and dad. Thank you to my father, Delatorro L. McNeal, Sr. I am so proud of you! Thank you for blessing me with a name that represents greatness, destiny, and determination. I am your namesake therefore, I am blessed with the challenge to take everything that you have done, and use it to an even greater degree.

To my mother, Olivia B. Fatherly. Wow, what can I say? The three musketeers have done it again! Thank you for teaching me about my speaking gift at an early age. Thank you for "holding on" in spite of. Thank you for giving up so much so that I can could gain the world.

To my older brother, Michael T. McNeal. Thank you for helping to raise me into the man that I am today. Thanks for paving the way and taking the spankings that I should have gotten. You are one of the few people who has always had my back. Love ya man!

To my mentors Les Brown and Willie Jolley. You know, they say that when the student is ready, the teacher shall appear. Well, God blessed me with both of you, almost at the same time. I could not ask for better mentors, friends, and fathers in the speaking industry. Whenever, I speak, coach, write, or consult – both of your spirits are with me, encouraging and supporting me. Thank you!

To my first home church, St. John Progressive M. B. Church. I can truly say that I owe a large portion of my speaking talents and confidence in my gift to speak to you. Since I was a baby boy, each of you encouraged me, supported me, and told me I would be somebody special. Praise God for each of you, and thank you Pastor Banks for allowing my gifts to flourish at a young age. You never held me back; you always helped push me forward.

To my home church, Without Walls International Church! Pastors Randy & Paula White, and the entire WWIC Family. WE DID IT! Not I did it, but WE DID IT! To each and every Pastor, Staff Member, Volunteer, MPIP Intern, FYI, MG, and Man2Man member, I want to say Thank You from the bottom of my heart for seeing a gift in me, and investing prayers, words of encouragement, opportunities, finances, smiles, and lots of love. Thank you for ministering to Nova and I. This project would not have been possible without you.

To a man who invested in me, because he saw the vision. To a man who selflessly contributed many hours of voluntary work, editing, and creativity to my dream – because he believed in me enough to ACT on his belief. To the man who gave me the idea to write this book, and who helped it materialize much faster then I could have ever dreamed. Rev. Ricc Rollins, words cannot express the level of gratitude I have for your love, support, and investment of time, sweat, and creativity towards my vision of motivating millions across this world.

To several men who have had a tremendous impact on my life, the world needs to watch out, because these gentlemen are destined for greatness. Omega Forbes, Matthew Bonnett, Earl Davis Jr., Tallie Gainer, III, Rodlin Davis, and Cory Burgess.

To several men and women who have served as extended moms and dads to me. James Evans, Dr. Lee Jones, Dr. Naim Akbar, Dr. Brenda Spencer, Dr. Lou T, Dr. Kristen Davis-John, Dr. Reggie Jackson, and Dean Joy Bowen, Dr. Felicia Jordan, and Dr. John Payne.

To my sixth grade teacher, Mrs. Diane Williams, who taught me how to recognize my weaknesses as strengths waiting to happen. Thank you for teaching me the importance of purpose, potential, power, and education. Your investment in me will have everlasting ripple affects in the lives of millions across this world.

To the mentors that I have never met, but whose coaching, teachings, and character have changed my life; Bishop T.D Jakes, Dr. Miles Monroe, Bishop Noel Jones, Anthony Robbins, Oprah Winfrey, and Denzel Washington.

To all those who said I that I could not make it. To all those who said that I would never write a book. Thank you. Your negativity fueled my passion, power, positivity, and productivity, which empowered me to complete this project. God Bless!

To the Organization Development & Training Staff at the University of South Florida. Collectively, you all are the best group of professionals I have ever worked with. Thank you for allowing me and encouraging me - to be me, and to spread my wings in the academic and administrative arenas of the university. I love each of you dearly, and I pray Jabez blessings upon each of your lives.

Foreword by Les Brown

Get ready to transform your mind and elevate your life. The spiritually inspired gems in this book when read, contemplated, and internalized daily; will positively impact every area of your life. The words on these pages will provoke you to think, and challenge you to act and live your truth. You have greatness within you. Start each day knowing that there is far more to you, then you have been demonstrating, or could ever imagine. Use this book as a tool to release the greatness that is within you. This has been Les Brown, Ms. Mammie Brown's baby boy. God Bless!

"This book presents the type of daily food that elevates the mind, nourishes the soul, and feeds the body. A must-read for all those who are serious about intrinsic motivation."

Dr. Lee Jones
Professor, Administrator, National Orator
Florida State University

"God is no respecter of persons, but He is a respecter of principles. This book is loaded with powerful, practical, and spiritual principles that are sure to start you on your way towards greatness. Enjoy these 101 quotations, but most of all, apply the daily affirmations, and we guarantee that you will move from existing efficiently...to living abundantly!"

Drs. Randy & Paula White
Senior Pastors,
Without Walls International Church
Tampa, Florida

"Wow! This book is a must-read and a must implement, for anyone who is seeking to possess the attitude and accomplishments of a Champion. The 101 Gems in this powerful and practical book, are indeed priceless!"

Earl Davis, Jr.
The Man with the Champion Attitude
Speaker and Coach

"Delatorro is already a sage as a young man. 101 Gems of Greatness is inspired and refreshing wisdom to live by for persons seeking to experience the best life has to offer and to give the best of themselves."

Dr. Kristen Davis-John
Licensed Psychologist

Author Foreword

Dear Friend,

Empowered Greetings! I am honored that you have taken the step to invest in your greatness by reading this book. Whether you were given this book as a gift, or if you purchased it for yourself, I want to thank you for inviting me into your life. You know, the old saying says "Sometimes we don't pick the books we read, the books we read - pick us!" and I firmly believe that. It is not by accident that you are holding this book in your hands right now, its all a part of destiny. God's divine plan for our lives.

You know the Bible says that there is nothing new under the sun, so for me to say that all 101 quotes are 100% original would be untrue, so if you read something that sounds somewhat familiar, GREAT! That's confirmation that the quote and the affirmation need to become a part of your daily routine.

I do want to share with you that these quotations and affirmations represent the core of who I am and what I stand for. I was inspired to write these thought forms while in a myriad of different settings; in high school, in college, in corporate, in academia, in the boardroom, in the bedroom, in the airport, in the car, in church, in the gym, in the grocery store, in the mall, in the hospital, in the inner city, in the movies and the list goes on and on. You see, in order for us to transition from goodness to greatness, we must renew our minds DAILY wherever we are. Therefore whatever is uplifting, positive, empowering, encouraging, energizing, rejuvenating, motivating, and transforming...we must think on these things.

I challenge you to not only read the quotes and affirmations, but also to post them in your home and office, email certain favorites to family and friends, and most of all APPLY what you learn to your DAILY ROUTINE. In order to reap the benefits of greatness, you must be willing to pay the price of APPLICATION. Wow, that's another new quote right there...well, it's obviously time for me start working on quote book #2, so in the meantime, enjoy this book, email me with your support, and most of all LIVE what you LEARN.

Living my dreams, and helping you live yours,
The Greatness Guy

1.

Don't let the folk you hang with, be your hang up. But allow the people you connect with, be your hook up.

Affirmation

Today, I will choose to surround myself with positive, quality, special people whom I can develop and who will develop me.

People

2.

The people with whom you network will ultimately determine your net worth.

Affirmation

*Today, I will meet someone new.
Someone whose natural gifts can
help me to become a more profitable servant.*

3.

Presentation without Relationship is just Information. Presentation with Relationship brings Revelation.

Affirmation

Today, I will realize that when I open my mouth, I tell the world who I am. From today forward I will seek relationship first and information second.

4.

Right now there are two types of individuals in your life - Dream Developers and Dream Destroyers.

Affirmation

Today, I will separate my friends, colleagues, and associates into these categories... and quickly discard the destroyers before they try to kill my dream.

What type of person are you?
Are you one to:
Make things happen,
Watch things happen, or
Wonder what happened?

Affirmation

Today, I choose to be an action-oriented person. Life will not act on me;
I WILL ACT ON LIFE!

Your reality is comprised of two things - your actuality and your possibility!

Affirmation

Today, I will surround myself with people who will help me transcend my current reality and help me envision my possibility.

2.

It's God's job to bring positive people into our lives; it's our job to keep them!

Affirmation

Today, I am thankful for the blessings of positive people in my life! And today I will show my appreciation by expressing my love in a tangible way.

8.

Sometimes the vicissitudes of life can bankrupt your bank account of belief.

Affirmation

Today, I will allow others to make direct deposits of positivity into my bank account of life.

Don't let the People, Problems, and the Pain of your Past - Pause your Present, Punish your Person, Prison your Potential, and Paralyze your Progress.

Affirmation

Today, I will begin walking boldly into my future and not allow others to hold me back.

Some individuals may be certified and bonified, but if they can't see your vision, they are not qualified to facilitate your dream!

Affirmation

Today, I will watch for people who have the credentials, but not the character to help me live my dreams.

Don't just "Have a great day." but rather,
"Create a Fantastic Day!"

Affirmation

Today, I have the power to create the day that I want. I choose to create a successful and prosperous day!

Seizing the Day

101 Gems Of Greatness - Seizing the Day

Allow the knowledge of your Past, and the hope for your Future, to give you power and passion for your Present.

Affirmation

The three tenses of my life should be used to empower me. Today, I will pull the strengths from my past, present, and future to create a great day.

13.

Time is the great equalizer; it puts each of us on level playing field. Hit homeruns daily by maximizing your dash.

Affirmation

Today, I will hit a homerun on the playing field of life by simply utilizing my dash to it's fullest!

14.

Today - the present, is in the bloom of time.
Spring into each day with excitement,
expectation, and enthusiasm.

Affirmation

*Today, I have something or
someone to be excited about.
Today I expect great things to happen
to me! Today I will autograph my
endeavors with enthusiasm.*

Where you've been does not equal where you're going, as long as where you are is greater than where you've been.

Affirmation

I will do something different today that I did not do yesterday, to make tomorrow twice as better than today.

Time isn't something you have;
it's something you are given.

Affirmation

Today, I am blessed with 24 Hours,
1,440 minutes, and 86,400 seconds to be
all that I was born to be!

Time isn't something you schedule; it's something you seize.

Affirmation

*The average human spends
2 years of life waiting in lines
3 years of life sleeping
5 years of life driving
13 years watching television
17 years of life in school*

Today, I chose to seize all my spare moments and to make the most of each day I am blessed to occupy!

18.

Within today lies: your opportunities, your victories, your challenges, your struggles, your blessings, your greatness, your chances, and your possibilities. Now is your time, Maximize Your Moments!

Affirmation

Today, I will do all that is within my power to get out of me everything that God placed inside me!

Check your baggage at the Past; book your flight in the Present; and travel boldly into your Future.

Affirmation

Today, I will let go of my old challenges, embrace my existing success, and create my possibilities for tomorrow!

20.

Bless others with the three T's - your Time, Talents, and Treasures.

Affirmation

Today, I will invest these three assets into the lives of others who will be blessed by them!

Giving

I read a quote one time that said,
"Service is the rent we pay, for the space that
we occupy!" My question to you is,
"Are you up on your rent?"

Affirmation

*Today, I will humble myself and help facilitate the
dream of someone else, because I
realize that what I make happen for someone else,
God will make happen for me!*

Give your best, not your mess.
Give your last, not your trash.
Give from your heart from the very start.
Give today and don't delay!

Affirmation

Today, I will be genuine about the service that I provide for others. I will serve each client with quality and excellence.

Earn a Living, Live a Life, and Change a Life!

Affirmation

Today, I will work smart to earn my paycheck, spend time enjoying the gift of life, and use my talents to positively impact a life!

To each of us is given a primary gift.
This gift is like the trunk of your tree of life.
Out of the abundance of that primary gift,
the branches of your talents and
abilities will sprout!

Affirmation

Today, I will realize that each of my gifts have a common thread – my purpose. I will walk in my purpose to impact others lives today.

25.

There are people right now who are hurting, lost, confused, troubled, and living below their potential. These people are waiting on you to use your gift to help them.

Affirmation

Today, I will get up and get off the seat of "do nothing" realizing that my gifts can bring healing today… but only if I use them!

26.

Problems and trials in our lives are similar to the curveballs that pitchers throw in the game of baseball. However, without the pitch you could never hit a homerun!

Affirmation

Today, I will view each challenge as an opportunity to grow, develop, and mature.

Life's Challenges

Life's challenges are strength-builders
for later struggles we will encounter.

Affirmation

*Today, I will realize and embrace the fact that
nothing will be placed on me that with
Him I cannot handle.*

View your challenges as refining tools for excellence.

Affirmation

Today, I decide that my betterment is life's mission; therefore, my struggles are only testaments of my greatness being birthed.

Had you not gone through what you went through on Monday,
Friday might have wiped you out!

Affirmation

Today, I will understand that each problem I face builds my momentum and confidence for the problems I will face tomorrow!

101 Gems Of Greatness - Life's Challenges

Problems in life are like problems in mathematics; they all have solutions.

Affirmation

Today, I will focus on the SOLUTION, and the problem will soon disappear!

The process of moving from goodness to greatness is like baking a cake.
All the ingredients you need are inside you, but in order to go from batter to cake,
life must turn up the heat.

Affirmation

Today, I will withstand the heat so that I can become great in the process.

The companion to a life of daily action is a life of relaxation. The goal is balance - burn brightly, without burning out!

Affirmation

Today, I will leave work early or take an extended lunch break and do something just for ME! I deserve a reward, and today I will get it.

33.

Whatever didn't kill you -
was meant to craft you.

Affirmation

Today, I will see life as a master craftsman, molding me into the person I should be.

Whatever didn't take you out –
was meant to take you up.

Affirmation

I'm still here…so that means life did not win over me, I WON OVER LIFE and that makes me higher today then I was yesterday.

35.

Whatever didn't take you under –
was meant to carry you over.

Affirmation

Today, I will use the right attitude to view struggles in life not as creatures trying to pull me down, but as blessings trying to push me up!

Whatever didn't cause you to die – was meant to help you survive.

Affirmation

Today, I will pray that my illness or the illness of someone else will be cured and that double health will be restored.

37.

Whatever didn't mutilate you –
was meant to motivate you!

Affirmation

Today, I may feel pulled in many different directions, but what that really means is that I am very special, important, and irreplaceable! This world needs me.

38.

Meditate on the meaning of mentally motivating messages!

Affirmation

Today, I will take inventory of everything that enters my ear gate, eye gate, and mouth gate. All three should be positive and healthy for me.

39.

You must get rid of the waste,
that's taking up valuable space, in this place.

Affirmation

Just as I have to take out the trash in my home, today I will eliminate as many negative mental habits I can and replace them with positive ones.

Don't complain about the rain; because you were engineered to soar above the clouds.

Affirmation

Today, I will focus on using my positive mental attitude to increase my altitude, which will allow me exist at peace above my present challenges!

41.

Your attitude is the way you view your experiences, your environment, your obstacles, your opportunities, your rights, and your responsibilities.

Affirmation

Today, I will take a check up from the neck up and make sure that I am viewing all aspects of life through healthy lenses!

42.

Continually cultivate and consume, critical confidence-creating concepts.

Affirmation

Today, I will type and post 10 of my favorite quotes in this book and give them to 20 of my co-workers!

43.

Faith is the key ingredient to having a larger vision of yourself. It's kinda like what water is to kool-aid. It's kinda like what flour is to cake. And it's kinda like what ham hocks are to collard greens.

Affirmation

Today, I will fortify my dreams and ideas with the faith to believe that they will come to pass!

If in your mind you can conceive it, if in your heart you believe it, although your eyes may not see it, you'd better make ready to receive it, because through Christ you can achieve it!

Affirmation

Today, I will prepare my mind, heart, and hands to receive the blessings I cannot see.

45.

Vision allows you to get a sneak preview of your future. If you don't like the preview of your tomorrow, re-write your script today.

Affirmation

Since today is the tomorrow that I thought about yesterday, today I will do something to improve my tomorrow.

46.

Wherever you are in life, be like
Wendy's and Biggie size it!
Be like MacDonald's and Super size it!
Be like Burger King and Up size it!

Affirmation

Today, I will look at my existing goals and desired outcomes and I will double them. In addition, today I will double the action I need to take in one order to achieve them.

47.

There are five types of vision; eyesight, mind-sight, hindsight, insight, and foresight.

Affirmation

Today, I will use what I have learned from my past (hindsight) to make educated decisions in my present (insight), to greatly improve my future (foresight).

48.

Vision transcends your current situation and takes you to where you are going to be.

Affirmation

Today, I will not look at my here and now, but rather I will focus on the places I want to go.

49.

A goal is something you have, but a Vision is something that has you! It won't let you go until you realize it. It won't turn you loose until you achieve it!

Affirmation

Today, I will recognize and appreciate "the hold" that my vision has on me, and I will take a positive action step to feed it!

Your goals, dreams, aspirations, and visions are looking to you to give them life. Don't let death take you, with your greatness never achieved.

Affirmation

Today, I will give birth to a new idea or action item that will move me one step closer to my destiny.

51.

We all have an ID an "Individual Destiny". The sad thing is that most of us would rather walk around with fake ID's.

Affirmation

Today, I will attempt to answer these questions;

What is my ID comprised of?
Who am I?
Why am I here?
Whose life will be blessed because of my existence?

Purpose

In order to be ALL THAT, you must first become ALL THAT God intended when He created you.

Affirmation

Today, I will take my eyes of my material possessions, and focus my energies towards using what God has deposited inside of me.

53.

Don't live your life trying to be "the next" anybody. BECOME THE FIRST YOU!

Affirmation

Today, I will celebrate my uniqueness and EMBRACE the aspects of my character that make me special.

54.

What a tragedy to die a cheap copy instead of a priceless original.

Affirmation

Today I will focus on honing the gifts that make me different from those that I am normally compared to.

55.

The reality is that many of us are fiddling with our future, shucking and jiving with our success, dilly-dallying with our destiny, and playing with our potential.

Affirmation

Today, I choose to get serious about my life, my qualities, my endeavors, and my opportunities. To soar like an eagle, I can't act like a turkey!

Regardless of your problem, pain, or pitfall, you still have purpose, potential, and power!

Affirmation

Today I choose to have an attitude which says, "For everything about me that is negative, I have two aspects about me that are positive." Starting today, I will use my strengths to counteract my weaknesses!

57.

Proactively pursue your passion in life.

Affirmation

Today, I realize that the amount of energy that I expend towards the pursuit of my dreams, equals the amount of desire I REALLY have for my dreams.

58.

Purposely place yourself in positions to profit.

Affirmation

Today, I will deliberately, intentionally, and knowingly put myself in an atmosphere that will cause me to benefit.

The acquisition of knowledge, without the application of knowledge, is just like "faith without works" – it's dead!

Affirmation

Today I make the final decision to "Do What I Know." All the new information that comes into my life, will go right back out in a new life application.

Knowledge

When you don't know, never be afraid to ASK!
Actively
Seek
Knowledge

Affirmation

From today forward, I will operate on an ASKING mentality.

If I Ask, It shall be given to me!
If I Seek, I shall find it!
If I Knock, the door shall be opened!

In life, it's not the type of job you have, but rather the knowledge, skill, attitude, and passion with which you perform - that makes you a professional.

Affirmation

Today, I will continue to or begin to autograph my work with excellence. I will seek ways to become the best at what I do.

Goodness is free; Greatness will cost you! Are you willing to pay the price?

Affirmation

Today, I will strive for greatness not fame. For I realize that everyone who is famous is not great. And everyone who is great, is not famous!

Destiny

The distance between the first floor and the second floor is great, but the steps in between are very small. It is little action, done consistently, that leads you to your destiny.

Affirmation

Today, I will begin being faithful and consistent over the small things in my life, knowing that if I am diligent over the little things, eventually I will be a master over the big things.

64.

The keys to unlock your destiny lie within you!

Affirmation

Today, I will stop looking around me for success. Today, I will stop looking outside myself for keys that are in my own pocket. Today, I will realize that winning does not start around me - it starts INSIDE me.

You + God = Best Tag Team Possible

Affirmation

Today the most powerful teamwork strategy is when I have faith in myself and faith in God to the point to where I know that I can accomplish all that is within my power. But when my knowledge stops and my ability stops, that's when God begins and carries me much further.

When pursuing your dreams, the effort is up to you, but the outcome is up to God.

Affirmation

Today I will take action on everything that is within my power of influence, knowing that once I have done everything that I can, then and only then can I truly stand and wait for God to show up...and show out!

The game of life is a lot like the sport of football. You are the receiver, God is the quarterback, and the ball is your blessing. Positive people are your offensive line, and the end zone is your destiny.

Affirmation

Today, and everyday I will realize that God wants me to win! I was born for it. Therefore if I simply run the plays He calls, I will score touchdowns all life long.

Success in life is manual, not automatic.

Affirmation

Today, I will embrace the fact that true success is a deliberate, determined, and detailed choice that I must make for myself.

Don't wait for opportunities to be handed to you. Be proactive and go out there and pursue the opportunities you want.

Affirmation

Today, I will take 3 strategic power steps that will help create an opportunity that I have wanted.

70.

Opportunity will knock if you put a door there!

Affirmation

Today, I will bait the hook of opportunity and cast my net into the sea of possibility knowing that I will catch my big BREAK!

71.

Opportunity will show up at your doorstep - as soon as you give it an invitation!

Affirmation

Today, I will begin intense preparation for the opportunity that will come knocking on my door at any moment…knowing that opportunity always takes 'now' for an answer!

72.

Market your strengths, or society will assume your weaknesses.

Affirmation

Today, I will tell 20 people one major thing that I am good at. I will proactively share my gifts with everyone I encounter!

73.

Society has labeled today's youth - "Generation X". "X" being the mathematical symbol for the unknown. They labeled us "Generation X" because they have no clue who we are or what we would become. Well, society may not know who you are, but I do.

Affirmation

Today, I will take every negative label that has been placed upon me, and I will turn it into a positive motivating force in my life.

74.

You're "Generation Excellent" because you rise above every challenge.

Affirmation

Today, I will realize that every obstacle is my opportunity to rise above my current level and transcend to the next level.

You're "Generation Excessive"
because you go above and beyond.

Affirmation

Today, I will move from mediocre, nominal, and ordinary - to maximum, phenomenal, and extraordinary.

76.

You're "Generation Exclusive" because you're one of a kind.

Affirmation

Today, I will carry myself with the understanding that I am the BEST thing that I've GOT GOING. I am in the process of becoming the best me that will ever be.

77.

You're "Generation Excited" because the Joy of the Lord is your strength.

Affirmation

Today, I will look towards heaven and realize that my true strength does not come from what I eat or what I do, but from my relationship with God who loves me dearly.

You're "Generation Exemplary"
because you set the standard.

Affirmation

I will live today and everyday with the understanding that what I do today, sets the benchmark for the things that will happen tomorrow. Today, I choose to set high standards of excellence.

79.

You're "Generation Expensive"
because you were bought with a price.

Affirmation

Today, I will live my life with a greater since of urgency. I will realize that the reason I have the comforts of today, is because someone paid the price for them yesterday. Today, I will be grateful for the sacrifices others have made.

80.

You're "Generation Explosive" because you make a dynamite impact.

Affirmation

*From today forward, I will begin to allow what's inside of me to not just come out...But also **explode out!** I will explode my gifts, talents, abilities, and skills on my school, home, church, sports teams, and community.*

81.

You're "Generation Expressive" because you show how you feel.

Affirmation

Today, I will STOP WEARING the mask. I will begin to show the real me, the true me, the blessed me, the powerful me, the unique me, the destined me, the only me. The BEST ME!

You're "Generation Exuberant"
because your future is so bright.

Affirmation

Today, I will realize that although my past might have been clouded by calamity, my future is glowing with greatness! I will realize that my tomorrow, my next move, my next relationship, my next educational achievement will light up this world.

83.

You're "Generation Extravagant" because the average just won't due for you.

Affirmation

Today, I will decide that I am not satisfied with ordinary and average, results. I will only be satisfied when I reach my personal best!
I am only racing against myself!

You're "Generation Extraordinary"!
You're "Generation Extra Blessed"!
You're "Generation Extra Special"!
You're "Generation Extra Awesome"!

Affirmation

Today, I will operate from the paradigm that the only difference between the ordinary and the extraordinary…is a little extra. I will give that little extra more and more each day.

85.

Compelling reasons are the fire that keep the flames of your dreams burning brightly.

Affirmation

Today I will not allow the waters of wandering doubt - extinguish my enthusiasm, excitement, and energy!

Compelling Reasons

Your reasons are the most powerful alarm clock you have.

Affirmation

Today I will use my reasons to motivate me to rise early in the morning and seize the day!

Your reasons will be your backbone of support when you feel crippled by the weight of an unsupportive environment.

Affirmation

Today, I realize that not everyone will support my dreams. However, I will hold my reasons, my "whys" as the bridge that will get me from where I am, to where I want to be!

Your reasons will keep you company
when no one else is around to help you
achieve your goals.

Affirmation

Today, I will realize that when I am alone, I'm actually NOT alone. My reasons are looking over my shoulder, smiling at my progress and accomplishment.

Your reasons will be there to congratulate you when you reach your destination.

Affirmation

Today, as I accomplish my goals, I will look at the finish line and high-five my reasons, which have been my biggest cheerleaders all along!

Fervently Fight those Fickle Forces, that
Frequently Frustrate your Faith,
and Facilitate your Fears.

Affirmation

Today, I will build momentum. I will not allow the demon of doubt, nor the felon of falsehood stop me from claiming everything that God has for me.

Living Your Dreams

Hold on to your dreams, even when you are experiencing nightmares.

Affirmation

Today, I will look past my present circumstances and remember that I am pregnant with a dream that will not die; and if I hold on, and if I do not faint, my dream WILL come TRUE!

Not being satisfied is the prerequisite to greatness!

Affirmation

Today I realize and recognize that I want more out if life. I want to do more, I want to be more, I want to love more, I want enjoy life more. Goodness does not satisfy me, I am hungry for greatness!

93.

The proverbial glass is not half full, nor is it half empty - it's both! At the same time!

Affirmation

Every day of my life I will exist as full and hungry simultaneously. Pleased with my today, but full of expectation for a better tomorrow!

Possession of and occupation of
your current level, allows you to be full;
but the desire for and anticipation of the next
level allows you to be empty!

Affirmation

*Today, I acknowledge the greatness that is within
me! I honor it, I feel it, and I celebrate it! I will use
my present to feed my future!*

Greatness mandates that you have a paradigm shift to the point that you make your success mandatory, not optional.

Affirmation

Today I will operate under a new mental framework.

Mandatory
Fulfilling my Purpose
Maximizing my Potential
Releasing my Power
Being an Effective Leader
Walking in Integrity
Striving for Greatness

Optional
Fulfilling Others Expectations
Maximizing my Wardrobe
Releasing my Opinion
Being Popular
Keeping up with the Joneses
Seeking Fame
Being in the Spotlight

Don't let the Lid of Limitations -Lock you out of Living, Learning, and Loving Life.

Affirmation

Today, I recognize that there are many challenges that have attempted to keep me meandering in the maze of mediocrity. Today, I will begin to turn each challenge into the combination that will unlock my DESTINY!

Your life story is housed within your chronological assets, not your financial assets.

Affirmation

Today, I will begin to minimize my chronological liabilities and maximize my time; this will yield my greatest financial breakthrough. Today I will give myself a raise by utilizing my time more wisely.

That extra heartbeat that you feel in your spirit craving for more; that's your destiny calling you. You better click over!

Affirmation

Today, I will hang up with negativity, and click over to positivity. It will be best conversation I will ever have.

It's not racism, it's not socialism, It's not sexism, it's not capitalism, It's not collectivism, and it's not materialism…It's YOUism!

Affirmation

Today, I will realize that I am my greatest gift and my greatest challenge. It's not anyone or anything else. It's ME! If it is to be, then it is UP TO ME!

Principles that guide our lives are similar to the formulas of mathematics. Once you know the formula, you can solve any problem!

Affirmation

Today, I will apply the principles of Loving, Giving, Visioning, Revising, Sharpening, Serving, Praying, Investing, Leading, and Learning to solve my present and future challenges.

101 Gems Of Greatness - Living Your Dreams

New Information leads to…
New Revelation leads to…
New Activation leads to…
New Transformation!

Affirmation

Today, I will allow the power of new information to cause a ripple affect in my life that will ultimately lead to Lasting Positive CHANGE!

Today, I will email Delatorro and let him know the impact his book has made on my life.

Today, I will make an investment in someone else and purchase this book for them, sign it, and encourage them to go to the NEXT LEVEL with me!

Final Thought from Delatorro L. McNeal, II

You were **born** to be the **bomb,**

You were **travailed** to **triumph,**

You were **conceived** to **contribute,**

You were **cherished** to be a **champion,**

You were **birthed** to be a **blessing,**

You were **delivered** to go after your **destiny,**

and

You were **nurtured** to **navigate** your course!

To order additional copies of
101 Gems of Greatness
Photocopy this order form and mail it along with your check or money order to:
A Noval Idea, Inc.
P.O. Box 27242
Tampa, FL. 33623
Or You can fax credit card orders to (813) 960-1556 To order online please visit our website at www.delmcneal.com

Name: _____ Phone: _____

Address: _____

City: _____ State: _____ Zip: _____

Quantity	Description / Title	Unit	Total
	101 Gems of Greatness	$15.00ea	
	Keys to Unlock Your Greatness CD	$15.00ea	
	Power Principles for Empowering Families LIVE Video	$20.00ea	
	Are You Willing? Audio Project	$15.00ea	
	Seven Steps to Greatness! Audio Project	$15.00ea	
		Sub-total	
		Shipping	
		Freight	$3.95*
		Total	

* Add $1.00 per additional product after two products Method of Paymen: ❏Money Order   ❏Visa   ❏MC   ❏AMEX
Credit Card #: _____

Expiration Date: _____

Signature: x_____
Please make all Money Orders and Checks Payable to A NOVAL IDEA, Inc.

To order additional copies of
101 Gems of Greatness
Photocopy this order form and mail it along with your check or money order to:
A Noval Idea, Inc.
P.O. Box 27242
Tampa, FL. 33623

Or You can fax credit card orders to (813) 960-1556 To order online please visit our website at www.delmcneal.com

Name: _____ Phone: _____

Address: _____

City: _____ State: _____ Zip: _____

Quantity	Description / Title	Unit	Total
	101 Gems of Greatness	$15.00ea	
	Keys to Unlock Your Greatness CD	$15.00ea	
	Power Principles for Empowering Families LIVE Video	$20.00ea	
	Are You Willing? Audio Project	$15.00ea	
	Seven Steps to Greatness! Audio Project	$15.00ea	
		Sub-total	
		Shipping Freight	$3.95*
		Total	

* Add $1.00 per additional product after two products Method of Paymen: ❏Money Order   ❏Visa   ❏MC   ❏AMEX
Credit Card #: _____

Expiration Date: _____

Signature: x_____
Please make all Money Orders and Checks Payable to A NOVAL IDEA, Inc.

For more information on Delatorro L. McNeal,

II and his motivational programs, products,

and services, contact:

A NOVAL IDEA, Inc.

P.O. Box 27242

Tampa, FL. 33623

Website:www.delmcneal.com

Email: info@delmcneal.com

Office: 1-866-GRATNES

Delatorro L. McNeal, II is the CEO and founder of A Noval Idea, Inc. and an Award-Winning Motivational Speaker, Author, Performance Consultant, and Success Coach. He partners with corporations, churches, educational institutions, and civic organizations across the nation to help transition them from goodness to GREATNESS!

Delatorro earned both his B.S. degree in Interpersonal and Speech Communication and his M.S. degree in Instructional Systems Design and Human Performance Enhancement Technology from the Florida State University. Delatorro and his lovely wife Nova, reside in Tampa, Florida and are faithful members of Without Walls International Church.

Affectionately known as "The Greatness Guy", he takes audiences across this country by storm with his powerful, practical, and prolific messagescentered around his mantra, "Goodness in free, but Greatness will cost you!

Are you ready to pay the price?"